A True Story of Love, Grief, Recovery, and
How Badly It CAN Suck!

BELLA LYNN THOMPSON

BROOKLYN
WRITERS PRESS

Copyright © 2020 Bella Lynn Thompson

Partially edited by Author Connections, LLC

All rights reserved.
Published in New York City by the Brooklyn Writers Press, an imprint of the Brooklyn Writers Co. LLC.

www.brooklynwriterspress.com

This book is a memoir, based on real events.

TITLE: Sudden Widow, A True Story of Love, Grief, Recovery, and How Badly It Can Suck!

ISBN: 978-1-952991–02-8 (e-book)
ISBN: 978-1-952991-01-1 (paperback)

Library of Congress Catalog Card Number: 2020910267

1st Edition

This book is dedicated to my late husband, my children,

and all those who have lost someone they loved.

TABLE OF CONTENTS

Dear Reader,

I hope this book gives you a bit of solace, and provides some meaning in belonging to a group we do NOT want to be members of. If this book answers a question and offers some healing, I will consider it a success. These pages might make you laugh and cry. My greatest wish is for this little book to help you realize a big thing—that even if your life is radically different from what you thought it would be, there is hope and value in surviving. Life is worth living.

With warm regards,

Bella

—CHAPTER 1—

LIFE BEFORE

People speak about adversity as if it's a good thing. I'm not sure that's the case. Many think the worst part of becoming a sudden widow is losing someone you love, but it isn't only that. Dealing with the ramifications that branch out in every direction, recognizing that life as you knew it is over, sucks!

Paul was by far the light of my life—gorgeous, funny, sweet, helpful, and as reliable as the sun rising and setting. He was an even better father than spouse, and easily impressed others with his kid-skills, not only with our own children, but entertaining most he knew or spent time with. Even dogs and cats liked him.

Don't get me wrong. My husband could be stubborn and a royal pain in the ass. He was not easy to live with, but given all of him I was way happier to put up with his shortcomings than live without him. We were together for twenty-one years, and 99.9 % of the time I would do it all over again, even knowing the outcome.

I didn't love my husband because he was perfect—he wasn't. But I wouldn't trade a minute, an hour, a day, or a year we spent together for anything. Even if I fleetingly thought about divorcing him every three to six months, and I would frequently tell him I was so angry I wanted to kill him, in truth, I could never.

Paul often joked about killing me (humor was by far his best quality). In fact, when one of my clients once threatened to hurt me, his response was, "There is no way he can want to kill you. That guy only spent eight hours with you. I've spent twenty years with you—who is he? If anyone has a right to take you out, it's me."

He joked about ending me after our second child was born. Barely two hours after I gave birth, his best friend came to visit. Without saying a word, Paul took the baby ever so gently from my arms and his friend approached me with a pillow, as if to smother me. They both said now that Paul had his two boys, my usefulness had expired. Then of course, they roared with laughter.

Paul and I met in a park, in 1994. He was riding his bike; I was jogging. We had each flirted with people we were interested in, and after seeing him around for a week or two, I noticed him standing on the side of the track with his bike.

My assertive personality took hold. I walked right up to him and introduced myself in a business-like fashion. I put my hand out to shake his, said my full name, my job title, and where I worked at the time.

He looked at me, kind of in shock. I think he would have preferred for us to smile at each other for a couple more days (or weeks), then let things happen organically; not a formal business introduction. He didn't know then that I have no patience. I prefer to plow to the next step, no tiptoeing. Organically let it happen? Really?

He was gorgeous, and as I jogged away from him I remember concentrating to make sure my butt looked good. I had no idea how to do this or if it worked, but it was my sole focus at the time. About ten minutes later, Paul rode up beside me and started chatting. His question was ridiculous; something like, "I see you like running, how far do you usually run?"

We spoke the whole time I ran and then spent the next few evenings together after work, meeting in the park and talking for an hour or two.

The next week, I hurt my knee and missed some evenings at the park. I remember the smile on his face when I came back a few days later, and in the sweetest voice, he said, "Where'd you go?"

I kept thinking, I don't know if this guy will ask me out on even one date, but if he does, I'm getting a picture, because he would be by far the most gorgeous man I've ever dated. He had the body of an underwear model, a beautiful smile with perfect white teeth, and sparkling hazel eyes against tan skin and dark hair. He was definitely my type.

He asked me out that night, even though we were both sweaty and disgusting from exercising, we went to a fast food place to get acquainted. Paul asked me what I wanted out of life. I gave him an earful—dreams, ambitions, where I wanted to live, etc. When I asked him the same question, his answer was simple.

> *"I want to fall in love, get married,*
> *have kids, and be happy."*

What a line! Seriously, I couldn't believe he really meant it; it was too good to be true.

Obviously, I was a bit cynical, because… fast forward… he meant it. After our first date, we saw each other almost every day until the day he died.

Paul liked me the way he met me, with no make-up and in yoga pants. Even on our wedding day, he looked at me sweetly and said, "What happened? Where's my bride? Why do you have all that stuff on your face? Why is your hair curly?" Yes, I wanted to punch him, but I thought, being myself without anything extra was beautiful to him, and that was an incredible feat. It made me feel wanted and appreciated both physically and as a person, emotionally and cognitively. That's why I married him.

I admit, it was a little disappointing on our wedding day that everyone was talking about "what a handsome groom" instead of "what a beautiful bride." Even so, it was perfectly fine with me. I always joked that he was prettier, and it was true.

He wasn't only the most handsome; he was also the favorite uncle, son-in-law, and brother-in-law. My family would tease me and say, "If there's a divorce, we're keeping *him*!" I was fine with that, and when there were hard times in our marriage, I always expressed to him that no matter what, he had me and my family. He didn't have a family of his own to fall back on; friends, yes, but not a nuclear family. Even if we were ever to divorce, my family and I would always be there for him.

In one of our worst fights ever, Paul started grabbing his clothes to pack and said, "That's it! I'm moving in with your parents!" I actually started laughing, and then we both laughed. I joked that he could get a great new life if he wanted to, but I wasn't going anywhere. He was stuck with me, for better or worse.

These moments were thankfully infrequent and fleeting in our marriage; maybe a few times over the years. When you truly love someone, you always try to think of them, what would be best for them, what would keep them safe and make them happy.

When I think about it now, I realize the decision to bury Paul alongside my parents made a profound statement. He alone, among their 'children' is buried with them. As I write this, I'm crying and smiling at the same time.

It's funny, as I think back, Paul was elusive at times. The first time I asked him for help, I needed a ride home from the train station, my unreliable car was in the shop. I let him know what train I was coming home on and he was supposed to be waiting. When he wasn't there, I thought to myself, I knew he was too good to be true. No one that gorgeous could be that nice!

I began walking home to my parents' house, hoping I could hitch a ride with them. As I crossed the street from the train station, I was walking past a building with mirrored windows and in the reflection, saw my Adonis… Paul was there.

I ran a marathon when I was in my late twenties. I had rage built up from earlier times in my life, and I was working it out by running. The marathon was a catharsis, some closure on that part of my youth. Paul was supportive. I trained for over a year in rain, cold, heat; it was a mission.

The day finally came, I was going to finish no matter what, and I was so proud of raising money for childhood cancer. In your body, every cell has memory. I don't know if everyone knows this, but they should. I ran almost a perfect nine-and-change-minute mile for 26.2 miles. Paul and his best friend were riding all around the city, following me intermittently. I remember seeing the finish line and wondering where I was going to find them. You're tired after a run of that length and I probably wasn't thinking clearly. I just wanted to see him.

I kept looking at the finish line poles, saying it was close, almost there, don't stop, don't stop. All the time, I was thinking if I *did* stop, I wouldn't likely start again! As I came within two feet of the finish line, I saw him from the corner of my eye. He had been tracking me for some time and we crossed the finish line together; me running, albeit slowly at that point, with him on his bike just outside the finish line bars. This is still by far one of the best moments of my life.

Paul was almost always an angel in my life. He was the one who brought me food at 4 A.M. when I was up writing my thesis, then dissertation. He was the one who would shut off the lights during midterms and finals and say, "You'll still get an A. Go to sleep already." He held my hand during difficult transitions, rough waters, challenges in graduate school and at work.

We waited to have our first child until I completed graduate school. Of course, he was there when I received my degree certificate. We had a party and it honored him as much as me, because it was clear that without him, I couldn't have accomplished this. He was my rock, my muse, my strength. My achievement in graduate school was ours to share.

Paul helped constantly when the boys were first born and afterward—changing diapers, staying awake endless hours when they were sick, entertaining them during the day and night when necessary, cleaning, shopping, whatever was needed. We truly worked together. Life wasn't easy, and who is it easy for? We both worked a lot.

The boys of course were a joy, well, if you have kids, obviously, I mean a joy *sometimes*. I thought Paul felt like they were a joy even more than I did. He was able to look at them with pure love, whereas I was marred and saw them in a loving yet realistic way. We were both full-time parents, but he spent more playtime with the boys than I did, especially after they each turned three and four years old.

No matter what, still in love after ten, fifteen, twenty years, Paul was still pinching and chasing me in playful ways, always professing his love in front of the kids. Despite arguing and disagreements, we always made up, and we were happy more than not.

There were no major issues between us—no infidelity, no alcohol or substance use, no selfishness or lack of caring. We only dealt with occasional differences of opinion, and that isn't enough to leave the love, friendship, and passion we had for each other. We both knew that.

When people ask about Paul, the smile on my face is so bright, they say it's remarkable. When I speak about times we spent together or funny things he would say, sometimes I still laugh out loud! He truly is the gift that keeps giving.

I recently saw the movie *The Boss Baby* (2017) and could almost hear Paul convincing the children that I came out of the womb wearing a suit and carrying a briefcase, with no apparent sense of humor, all business. He would likely attempt to convince my mother of the same, and as she has dementia—no joke—she would be easily convinced. I can hear her giggle as he would say it.

As for me, I have a Ph.D. and best qualify as a geek or nerd. I am studious, and if I had my druthers, I would go back to school despite having already spent more time in school than most people ever do.

My extensive time in the world of academia definitely influenced how I approached becoming a widow. Obviously, I don't like being a widow, but however you look at it, Paul was a gift to me for twenty-one years, and despite a sudden and unexpected, dreadful outcome, he provides me joy to this day.

—CHAPTER 2—

HEART TORN TO PIECES, THE DAY

Two months before Paul died, I told him marrying him was the best decision I ever made. The night before he died, I told him I loved him. On the morning of his death, it was a nice day, but he was cranky and not feeling well. I called out for him to come in from his endless manicuring of the lawn. It seemed like a normal enough morning.

It was the day of his best friend's wedding, and Paul was the best man. His friend was forty-six, it was his first marriage, and he had waited nine years to get married.

Paul asked why my elderly parents were coming to the church to see him as a groomsman. He thought it would be too much trouble for them.

"They would come to see me, so why wouldn't they come to see you? They love you like a son, they're coming to see you, so shut up about it!"

For a few minutes, when I could see he didn't feel well, I begged him to let me drive him to the doctor or even the hospital. But Paul was a man of his word, always did what he said he would do. He was a reliable person who would never disappoint someone or go back on a promise. He was also stubborn, and he was leaving to go and be there for his friend.

As they were taking pictures before the ceremony, Paul died suddenly of a heart attack. Thinking back on it now, it was far better that he died taking pictures before a wedding than in front of our home and our children. Our boys were nine and eleven-years-old at the time. There is never a good time for a dad to die, so I have little comment on his or their ages, besides that we all wish he had lived longer.

I will never understand why no one called me. I only found out Paul was at the hospital when I arrived at the church.

Driving to the hospital was the most horrific ride of my life. For many years, one of my greatest fears had been not making it to the hospital in time during an emergency for a loved one. I guess I always pictured one of my parents in need. Now I was panic stricken, driving in traffic, barely able to breathe, with both boys in the car.

I called my parents and told them to skip the church and go straight to the hospital. They called my brother, who called the hospital and then me, to say I must hurry and get there soon. I called the doctor in the emergency room and he said there wasn't much time.

***

At 2:38 PM, five minutes before we rushed into the hospital, I felt a presence in my heart or soul. I truly don't know what it was or how to explain it, but it was Paul. He let me know, *'It's over, and you're driving our kids.'* I knew it was him, and a calm came over me like he was holding me to get me through the next few hours.

I am still emotional that my husband, a man who was so loved by so many, died alone in the hospital. That day and the next few were the worst of my life.

When I got to there, I sprinted to the ER. A friend had

followed me to watch the boys in the waiting room. Paul was already dead when I arrived.

The staff asked to "clean him up" before I saw Paul, but I was adamant that I see him immediately. They allowed me to go in. He was still my beautiful husband, and I grabbed him and hugged his lifeless body as I cried.

Then I had to leave the emergency room and tell my children their father had died. How do you do that? What do you say? Paul played baseball with them constantly, and all I could think was that I would have to learn to play. I was in shock after being alone with Paul's body as I finally made my way to the waiting area.

My boys were dressed in their suits for the wedding and I was standing in my little black dress and high heels. I looked at them and said, "Daddy's gone. I'll try to learn to play baseball." My mother screamed, and my Dad, whom I had never seen cry in my entire life, began sobbing and left to go to his car.

I was so upset Paul was gone, I wanted to die. I wished it was me. He was the one who played with the boys all the time. He helped around the house; he got up with them when they were sick as much as I did. I couldn't grasp the harsh reality of having to live without him.

We had to wait at the hospital for hours. A detective came to interview me. I think I was a suspect at that point, or at least my playing any part in Paul dying had to be ruled out. It was a female detective. She looked at me and said, "I heard your husband was on his way to a wedding. How much partying did he do last night to die today?"

I was too overwhelmed to be livid, so I carefully took a breath, then spoke at length, calmly citing the facts. "My husband never tried smoking or an illegal drug in his life; he ate a low-fat salad every day for lunch for almost thirty years; he wouldn't eat junk food, wouldn't contaminate the temple of his body; he was physically active. We didn't even have alcohol in our house except for parties maybe twice a year. As a matter of fact, my husband was at a Home-run Derby, baseball practice for his nine-year-old and went to sleep by 10 P.M. last night. Oh, and he has been at the same job for almost thirty years, won attendance awards, and was respected in his workplace." *UUGGH!*

The officer quickly became civil and we finished up her questions soon after. In retrospect, this probably wasn't the best thing to say; however, at one point in the interview, I said, "Listen, if I killed him, it was from aggravation." Without skipping a beat, one of the other police officers said, "If that was the case, most husbands would be dead."

At times in the hospital, I was joking about Paul elbowing Jesus, saying, "See, she talked so much, it killed me." I imagined he would be laughing while saying it in Heaven. The joking was an unsatisfactory ruse to deflect any feeling, because if I took in any of what was happening at the time, I would have been in the fetal position on the floor, screaming in agony and crying. I did plenty of that, just not in public.

On the drive home, I lamented not getting there in time to see Paul before he died.

> My older son said,
> *"I know you would have
> died for him in a second, Mom."*

It's funny how comforting that statement was to me, and has remained so. John was right. I would have traded my life for Paul's without a thought.

My younger son, Mark, was in shock; he couldn't speak. Only three days after Paul died, I was on the phone with the insurance company agent who was interviewing me to ensure I hadn't killed my husband. Mark wanted to get to Paul so badly, he took a knife, and asked if he made all the blood leave his body, could he see his dad again?

The calm I felt on that first day slowly dissipated. For a few months, it was there intermittently, then sadly replaced by a zombie-like state of I don't know what. The kids were always fighting. My older son's Obsessive-Compulsive Disorder was off the rails, and my younger son simply didn't see the point of anything; he was most often in an apathetic stupor.

I was angry, enraged, and cried often.

—CHAPTER 3—

SUDDEN WIDOW: THE BEGINNING OF SUCKING AND THE AFTERMATH

In the beginning, I was shocked, in a fog, heartbroken, and at times wished I had crawled into the coffin with my husband.

Paul felt sick the morning he died, and for a time I blamed myself for not taking him to the hospital. After multiple conversations with the medical examiner, my initial guilt eased because what happened to Paul was a fatal event, not likely preventable that morning. He was forty-seven-years-old. I was forty-six.

First and foremost, I obtained seven years of previous medical records on Paul, to ensure I hadn't missed anything. Then, with help, I completed almost all the required paperwork following his death in the first five weeks. I returned to running and working out at the gym as a way to release the rage and grief that filled me. Although I've always been an avid exerciser, this was with a vengeance, hitting it hard about two hours a day.

For the record, two months before he died, with no indication he would be gone any time soon, I announced to him on my birthday that he was the best decision I ever made. Still true today!

The best part of being a widow is smiling when recalling a memory of Paul, or thinking of what he might say today. The worst part is all the CRAP I have to deal with and manage without my life partner and best friend. I miss him daily.

It's a miracle Paul put up with me. I'm obsessive, forever worried, and repeat myself often, especially when someone has the audacity to think I'm wrong. I'm usually correct—well, almost always, as a wife that is. As a practitioner, I believe I showed good judgment and suffered over all clinical decisions, always doing my due diligence and giving my work 110%. He would tease me and make fun of my shortcomings, but then always grab me, pinch my tush or hug me, and say how much he loved me. These memories are now priceless to me and still make me smile when I think of them.

The most unbearable part in all this, is seeing my children in pain. To see them missing him, crying, and having no way to fix it or deal with it is impossible.

The fallout cannot be overstated. Death changes everything. The trauma affects the entire family, even the extended family. It is too much to bear alone. Of course, we talk about Paul and the boys have been in bereavement therapy. I try to be supportive and do the best I can for them, but none of it is any kind of fix! It's a terrible process to watch as a parent. Their grief is added to my own, and even in my darkest moments, I know I must be strong for them. It truly sucks.

For the first several months, my children and I were running at a ten on a scale of one to ten emotionally. Before Paul died, 'stupid' was a curse in our house. After, the F-bomb became a regular part of our vocabulary. I freely admit this was my fault. I was grieving and exhausted.

The first two to three months, every night I ran from room to room, to comfort each child. I slept with my younger son, who fell asleep touching my shoulder to make sure I was there and alive. This went on for six or seven months, while my older son—who no longer slept at all—would wake me.

Life sucked for a long time, and yet, deep down, I was hopeful. I knew I would have a second life. Maybe I could fall in love again, get married, start a different life, still practice... maybe in a different environment.

My children were different now. My older son was angry and upset; in addition to not sleeping, he had no interest in school. This created a cascade of problems. The wonderful teachers, counselors, and administrators at school were constantly concerned and calling regularly. Meanwhile, my younger son was equally uninterested in school and seemed to lose most of any confidence he had in himself. It had started before Paul died and was amplified tenfold afterwards.

As a single parent, you need a break sometimes. You need to get away from the kids! I wish I had a full-time, live-in nanny. Jeez, I wish I had my own bedroom. I sleep on a couch.

My house has two bedrooms. One is my older son's, and I gave up our room for my younger son. As a mother I was constantly torn; wanting to provide structure and safety, yet needing to mourn and cry without interruption. It's manageable the first few months because of all the help, but following that, most people — even those with wonderful intentions — forget or may believe the problems are better, that you aren't in need of help any longer. Maybe they want to respect your privacy, or they simply want to get back to their own lives. Regardless of the reasons, the result is the same. You are left to your own devices.

Things can get out of hand! John and Mark were wrestling, and John, my older son was so angry, I thought he was going to kill Mark, maybe accidentally hurt him. I panicked and locked Mark and myself in our den. I held the door to the den as my five foot seven, one hundred and sixty-five pound son pushed the door open not once, not twice, but three times. I held my back against the door, then my hand. Finally, I was forced to pull John away from Mark with all the strength I could muster on my left side and arm.

I remember saying, "I think you've dislocated my shoulder." Who has time to check? We had multiple baseball games, both boys played on travel teams, and they were still arguing!

I waited ten days, trying to keep up with our hectic family schedule, until finally, I passed out from the pain and went to the hospital. They diagnosed a pinched nerve and sent me home. Five days later, I went to the doctor and had an MRI, which reported a crushed disc in my neck that was impinging on my spinal cord, and a fractured scapula. At this point, my hopes for a great new life were dwindling.

Just over a year after Paul died, I had surgery. I was cut from side to side and they took out about two feet of intestine due to an umbilical hernia, which by this point had been a longstanding problem. My cervical spine impingement happened just three weeks before this surgery, which complicated things.

While in recovery, even though laughing hurt and moving hurt more, I wanted to record video of myself, just for laughs. I have a dark sense of humor after all, and thought it was hysterical when I had to shimmy and slither my body using only my right side and right arm to move myself out of a seated position. I had no core muscles to use due to the stomach surgery, and my left side was unable to bear weight because of the fracture in my neck. I also lost feeling in my left forefinger, second finger, and part of my thumb from the door incident with the boys. I was in chronic pain; not just from the first surgery, but from my neck injury. Five months later, I needed neck surgery. It was as my friend would say, good times. I am proud of how I made it through that recovery and did so laughing, at least sometimes.

Six weeks after neck surgery, I had burning sensations on the lower part of my back, and a rash. I thought, *how weird, what now?* I finally went to the doctor and was diagnosed with… shingles. That wasn't too terrible in itself, but the medication they gave me for shingles exacerbated a long-standing autoimmune disease, which I had to take care of next. I stopped even telling people about the latter two issues, shingles and the autoimmune disease flare-up, because it started to sound unbelievably ridiculous, pathetic, and well, like, almost impossible.

People ask how I made it through that period of my life. The answer is, I had some help from friends and family, and I paid for help for myself and the boys. I express that if I could live through two surgeries while managing the boys without a significant other, it proved I could make it through anything. It was a significant test.

Little did I know, more tests were coming, as they do for all of us. The rollercoaster of trials and emotions would continue for many months.

—CHAPTER 4—

WANTING
TO SMASH THINGS

This is a short chapter, because it is self-explanatory. Now and then, I want to smash things, punch things, and generally destroy some things of Paul's. I frequently say that when I get to heaven or wherever he is, I'll punch him first and hug him right after.

I'm still angry he left, though much less now than right at the beginning. No, this is NOT what he wanted; and no, I don't think it's his fault! I'm just really pissed that he left me with everything!

I have all of his stuff. Well, I gave away a ton of his usable clothing, shoes, and coats in the first three months after he died. OMG Paul's idea of procrastination was if he said something needed to be done and it wasn't completed prior to him finishing the request or soon after, I was procrastinating. Therefore, waiting three months to give his clothes away, I'm sure he wanted to haunt me.

He left all this stuff—tools and other things for the house, plus an old vintage car that I referred to as a large paperweight for most of our marriage. His standard reply about that beloved car was, "I can get a new wife easier than a new car." This was true. We constantly joked about the value of his classic auto-baby.

I wanted to smash his gravestone, rip his pictures, throw the phone. I didn't do any of these things. Well, I did throw the phone once or twice. I was angry. I still am. It has subsided tremendously, but unlike what people perceive as the stages of grief, emotions sometimes erupt and flow like volcanoes, even after a long silence. Out of the blue, a new memory, a problem, or some painful issue might occur, and it feels like I am back to day one or month two, even after feeling better for a while.

I would equate this with getting hit by a Mack truck. There is no predicting when it will happen. I have become better at noticing certain triggers; however, others are unavoidable.

Two days before Christmas this year, Big J called. Big J was one of Paul's ex-girlfriends. By the time I met her their romance was ancient history, but they were still friends and I immediately liked her. I didn't have any way to reach Big J after Paul died; she had moved to another state with her husband. I thought about trying, but didn't know where to start. The only friend who might still be in touch with her was also dead.

When she called, I tried to be okay, but I had to tell the story like it was day one all over again. It felt like being hit by a Mack truck! I told her if there was anything I could send to ease her pain, I would—pictures of Paul, anything. I got off the phone and collapsed to the floor, crying, wishing I could leave this world.

The first Christmas, we were all in a fog. The second Christmas was the worst holiday we had to survive yet. I think next Christmas will be better.

Another Mack truck moment. I was at an MLB game soon after Paul died. We were truly blessed that the town I come from helped so much. I know we're lucky to live in such a wonderful community. At times, I had rides for the boys, meals, and a good friend arranged for high school baseball players to volunteer to play baseball with my boys for the first few months after Paul died. I was grateful.

One of the high school coaches gave us great seats for the game. It seemed, at least to me, like Paul had to be in attendance, because both boys were able to catch batting practice balls that went foul. What luck, what a great thing!

I didn't venture out much on my own when Paul was alive. Work, professional engagements, shopping, a night out with the girls here and there, sure. But most everything else, I did with him. Well, the moment someone tried to pick me up and they were nasty about it, drunk and behaving inappropriately in front of my children, that was a Mack truck moment! I realized I was alone.

I work out religiously, but I am 5'2" and 120-125 pounds; not yet a contender. I'm working on it. I handled the situation as my sarcastic self and the guy went away fairly quickly, no harm done. It was just a shock!

Paul was a big guy. If someone ever looked at me the

wrong way, he looked at them and they *stopped*. I never even thought about having a problem like that when my husband was alive. It sucked to be reminded again that my beautiful husband was no longer around. I never even noticed this was happening until Paul was gone.

—CHAPTER 5—

NOT CARING
ABOUT ANYTHING

WHO CARES, when the grand outcome is the same no matter what you do? Death isn't like divorce. It's certain, final, permanent. And when you realize how little control you have regarding the outcome of life, it's hard to care about things moment to moment.

Do I really need a shower today?
Does it matter if I get a job?
Any reason not to smoke (I'm going to die anyway!)?
Does it matter if I try?

These are thankfully moments, not days. I have taken a shower all but three days since Paul died, and count that as an accomplishment. Feeble, I agree, but an achievement nonetheless.

Things simply don't matter like they used to. Nothing impacts me as much as it did before, except of course the boys and their health, which was our top priority before Paul died, and hasn't changed.

Even now, it's still hard to process that Paul died of a massive heart attack. As I said to that detective at the hospital, he rarely drank, never smoked, never did drugs, and ate a low-fat salad nearly every day for lunch. My all-time favorite irony, in response to, "Don't you want to order a deep-dish meat lovers pizza tonight?" his reply for twenty-one years was, "Well *you* can get that, but I'm not putting that in this temple."

I can't help but think now, *Really? YOU died!*

Two months after Paul passed away, I ate a deep-dish meat lovers pizza with the kids. I'm still here. So what do we really control? *Why care?*

The truth is, we control precious little, but there are plenty of reasons to care. Mine are easy to identify: John and Mark. That's why I have to care. Honestly, if I didn't have children, I believe I would have just worked and cared the best I could for my clients, as I did before Paul died. Without the boys, work would have been my sole focus and reason to live.

John, Mark, and I all transiently enter and exit this phase of not caring. It happened more often in the first year following Paul's death, but still in the second year and even the third from time to time.

*When you survive this kind of trauma
and suddenly have to rebuild a
new life you never expected, and
do it without your partner, the only
thing you can do is continue to
put one foot in front of the other.
Some moments that is the best you
can do; you simply don't care to do
more, and it has to be enough.*

—CHAPTER 6—

SINKING

When I'm asked to describe how I truly feel… I feel like I'm sinking. On my bad days, it's just the kids and me in a vast ocean. I'm helping to keep them afloat; once in a while fighting off a shark for any or all three of us.

On good days, we are actually in a life raft, able to see land. Since Paul died, these days are few and far between. As time goes by, there are more and more of them returning.

I described to my best friend that when I am sinking with the boys, there are life rafts I can swim to—she is one, plus other friends, my sister, my parents, my brothers, my babysitter, my kids' psychologist, and my job. These are all rafts I swim to for help.

I sank the most after the first year. My heart was still crushed by Paul's loss, and then my best friend and I stopped talking for a while. It was as if the pieces of my broken heart left on the ground had been stepped on. In this period of reflection, I decided that I was doing things wrong, and actively tried to change my behavior. I really wasn't myself.

It finally dawned on me, why I was so slow after Paul died. I mean, *practically cognitively challenged*—everything was a burdensome effort. It's part of depression—losing concentration; and part of grief is feeling terribly exhausted and fatigued. It took me forever to think of doing things for myself.

When presented with issues in my profession or other problems, I was doing better; even getting close to my old self or some new sort of normal. When it came to personal connections, however, the circumstances were entirely different. I had to come to terms with getting sad and lonely, with possibly never meeting another man of my dreams. Too many variables beyond my control made the future uncertain at best, and it made me sink a bit, but that's life. I decided to control how I raise my children, hopefully where I work, and what I do to survive.

People may need a WHY? for this sinking analogy. Well, here goes. I wake up worried about the future—how to pay for college, how to keep paying for health insurance, a place to live, bills, etc. Paul enjoyed making fun of these moments.

He would say something like, "Okay, you stay up and worry about how to save thirty-thousand dollars. I'm going to sleep. We both have to work tomorrow."

When we were challenged the most financially, he would say, "It will all work out. We can live on love." We were in it together, a team to deal with everything. Since he died, it is just me. Since I was already an Alpha and a control freak, I usually made decisions anyway, but we always discussed them. Now, I alone carry the weight of every choice and every result.

Paul rather liked that I made decisions, because if something proved to be wrong, he could blame me. Honestly, I was fine with that, no problem. Any decision is usually better than no decision, and some decisions are invariably wrong no matter what.

Now, I wake up in a cold sweat, wondering how I am going to support two children alone. Most households have two earners and struggle. How am I going to do it by myself? What about the house, the car, unexpected expenses? My Lord, how am I picking the boys up at the same time from two different places three times a week? How am I going to get them a safe car? How am I going to afford car insurance for two boys when they are old enough to drive?

My financial future changed drastically when Paul died. I closed my private practice, because there was no way I could be there 110% for my clients and also be present for my children. We lost his pension, we lost our dream of selling our house to send the boys to college and then we would move into a tiny house together.

We lost our hope of having too much time together in retirement, trying to come up with hobbies rather than idly bickering, which by the way we found enjoyable. Now, even if I accomplish financial stability, I will have to work until my dying breath to maintain it.

The overwhelming responsibility of being in charge by myself made me feel as if I was in a tiny boat that was rapidly filling with water. I used to joke that marriage is rarely a problem, marriage with kids is the tough part. Back then, I wasn't a single parent. I never wanted to be a single parent.

I don't know if I would have had children if I knew I would be a single parent. It has made me think about the difference between a widow/er and a divorced parent. Sometimes people share custody. That made me realize that people who have a parent who isn't involved, who is alive and could help but doesn't... well, that's sadder than my predicament any day.

I told and still tell the kids that
I am strong as steel. I let them
know every day that I love them. I
express that they can be better, more
flexible, empathetic people because
their father died. In fact, it is their
job to be better. Problems in life
increase wisdom and endurance.
Challenges are not there to break
you, but make you stronger.

Despite my (ad nauseam) requests, my screaming—mostly to wake them up and get them to do things—my boys know I am their number one fan. I will advocate for them and would die for them in a second. Truthfully, this experience is even worse for them. Losing a spouse is terrible, but losing a parent at their ages is far more traumatic.

Holding their pain along with mine feels overwhelming. I'm used to managing a house, but I had help. I am self-reliant and self-motivated, but I'm not used to doing everything by myself. Who wants to be in this crazy life alone? Well, I am, and nothing can change that right now. Even if I were to meet someone, I would still be the only living parent to my children.

We used to tell the kids how lucky they were to have two parents who loved them. Now I say how lucky they are to have one parent who loves them still here, and a father who was one hundred percent involved and engaged until his final day on earth. Paul loved our boys to the moon. Many kids whose parents are still alive cannot say that. Even on the bad days, we must be grateful.

It's still easy to sink when I think about raising two boys without their dad. They used to play baseball constantly, but refuse to play with me. They say they're going to hurt me, so they rarely play outside of team events these days. This makes me sad.

Soon after Paul died, someone said, "You have to be the dad and the mom." I thought, *No, thanks. I have to be the best mom, period.* Like any parental role, it is all-encompassing. There is no way I can replace their dad. That's impossible. I recognize now how lucky they were to have Paul even for a short time. And I was lucky to have my children with him. John and Mark are two parts of him that I love unconditionally. They are, *usually!* my greatest gift.

Sometimes I sink because I'm being hard on myself. I don't think I've been grieving efficiently enough: I haven't met professional goals in the last two years, I feel lazy, like a loser. I never bounced a check in my life until Paul died; never was overdrawn in a bank account until he was gone. It's not like we didn't come close, but somehow, selling things, even some precious to us, working more hours, whatever it took, we always scraped by.

In reviewing the last two years, I am painfully disappointed in my personal accomplishments. I'm sinking. What have I been doing with my time? Oh, it's called surviving.

My older son, John, called me up to three times a day from school the first year, to make sure I was alive. His OCD (Obsessive Compulsive Disorder) became so exacerbated, it took over my house for months. Mark and I were lucky to survive. I made countless appointments, inquiries to help him, always trying not to ignore Mark for him...The minute John was in check, Mark would have a crisis. Jeez, he deserved it because it was so rare for Mark to have a crisis, I understood.

They both practically failed out of school the first year. I spent countless hours in meetings with teachers and guidance counselors, begging the boys at home to do homework, trying to balance their needs with their obligations. Of course, I got a tutor, but they didn't want to work with a tutor.

With emotions running high at baseline, everything was explosive; anger was the default. I was working out to reduce my rage. I even tried kickboxing, and the instructor told me I was too aggressive.

The boys and I talked about Paul often and openly. We even talked about me starting to date again. When I tried, they knew that every date I attempted, I wished it was their dad. I guess it was obvious. I cried before most dates.

I was sinking in every aspect of my new life; above water, but just barely. I worried all the time, for the boys and for myself. I believe now that I couldn't take in the trauma of what I lost, and the fact that I lost my whole future or what I thought my future would be. I had been expecting to do everything with Paul by my side. To accept that my future with him along with our dreams and any financial security were lost as well, was too much at once.

Yes, I am a widow and things are inexplicably different since Paul died. However, things were already tough before. My older son already had OCD. It just became worse because of the added anxiety. Both kids had attention deficit issues well before Paul died. These challenges have been exacerbated by his death and now having only one parent to help them. When I feel like I'm letting them down, that is when the sinking feeling is worst.

Note to self: I'm not really
sinking. It only feels like I am.

—CHAPTER 7—

THE WORST DAYS

Since Paul died, no one in the house sleeps well. John especially, bangs around at all hours. Our home is thirteen hundred square feet. You can hear everything anyone does. I'm sure I haven't slept through the night more than ten times in the last three years. I hope at some point I can invest in soundproofing. Lack of sleep can make any day the worst day.

Death changes so much. It isn't possible to put the pain of my sons losing their father into words. The current daily struggle on top of other issues that existed before, is now amplified and feels unbearable at times. I'm exhausted all the time.

Not long after Paul was gone, my boys were already talking about me finding a new guy. John, my older son, said, "But try to find someone who will come to my baseball games. That's important."

I haven't found someone to come to his games. John is still angry and sad about this. He doesn't want me to attend his games. He says it just reminds him his dad isn't there. I get it.

On the contrary, my younger son doesn't want to play a game without me. One of the worst days was when Mark woke up and wanted to play baseball with Paul. He was inconsolable. It broke my heart more than any other day besides the day Paul died. Trauma, pain, heartbreak, all at once like a tidal wave.

John's worst day was different. His OCD took over and he couldn't control himself. Obsessive-Compulsive Disorder is tough. Regardless of the disorder, for some people, when everything is out of control, they try to over-control their environment.

It's difficult for many parents to raise a tween. Having a tween who is angry and managing grief and trauma issues, has been especially challenging. On his worst day, John threatened suicide over his phone being taken away. He had locked himself in the bathroom with a knife.

I was one week out of cervical spine surgery, in a neck collar. The psychologist I had hired to speak with the kids was at the house. From 7AM until 8:30AM we tried to reason with John, to no avail. My whole body was in a panic, which of course I could not show. I tried not to cry when the police and then the ambulance came. I wanted to come out of my skin.

I begged the ambulance driver to take John to the best hospital. Thankfully, he did. John was on medication. His psychologist and I had just met with his team from school a week earlier. I kept saying, "I'm trying so hard, but still, here we are." One of the police officers heard me doubting, questioning, second-guessing myself and all that came before this point. He finally said to me, "You can't think like that. You're doing all you can. Thank God you are here and it's not worse."

John was discharged to his psychiatrist that same day. I and the psychologist, who is a blessing, were grateful and we all worked on a plan going forward together.

That was one of the worst days. However, at the hospital, I realized that John was alive and receiving help. His psychologist stayed with us the whole day. I was complimented by all for being so prepared.

Even in the darkest times,
we have to remain grateful.

Now is better than the first six months or even the first year. I was a zombie then; barely thinking or eating, barely breathing, praying to God I could see Paul for just a second. I was bargaining with my own soul for one look at his smile, one spoken word, anything. Every day was the worst day.

I still feel like whenever it is my time to die, as long as my children are settled and I know they will be okay, I'll be ready to see Paul again. I actually wish for death now and then, because the pull to be with him again is so powerful. I don't know if people discuss this, but I'm sure others feel it, especially on the worst days.

CHAPTER 8

UGH! HOW TO CONTINUE?
WHAT DO YOU DO?

My original plan, which has now been adjusted—maybe seven thousand times, was to have a short list of specific goals:

A **personal goal**: *be the best mom and provide a net of safety for my children, because they lost a tremendous measure of safety when they lost their dad, just like I did, so, be ever-present.*

A **spiritual goal**: *find some peace and flow, a new path toward feeling calm and comfortable with life.*

A **cognitive goal**: *excel in the knowledge of my profession, continue to learn.*

A professional goal: *reassess the most creative and strategic objectives for employment.*

A physical goal: *get into great shape. (Ideally, to bounce a quarter off of my abs and butt. I'd like to say I'm almost there, but in truth, not quite...it's nice to dream.)*

And finally...

A silly entertainment goal: *catch up on twenty-plus years of movies I missed through graduate school and my time in practice, both of which were all-consuming.*

Thinking of goals and writing them out seemed ridiculous to me at first. However, I have found that I can survive a bad day by completing just one goal. On the worst days, it is little more than watching a movie or going to the gym.

It's way easier to go to the gym when you think someone new may eventually see you naked. Quite horrifying to think about, but definitely a motivator! One great thing about being sad most of the time is that you don't have to worry about smile lines. Less future Botox. No, I haven't tried it. Yes, I am tempted to.

*We all grieve differently
and have unique,
individual needs post-trauma,
so how we recover and carry on
doesn't look the same for everyone.*

My social connections and reaching out to help others got me through the first two years without Paul. Everyone should try professional bereavement counseling and/or support groups. I did both. I found the groups hard to bear. People were still talking about WHY? Why did this happen to me? Why did my wife/husband die so young? I was past the WHY.

Do Not Get Stuck In The 'WHY?!'
*WHY? is like quicksand, a quagmire;
you may never leave. WHY? is an
unanswerable question. There is no
reason, or maybe some believe there
is, but don't get stuck in the WHY?
People never move on from there.*

Try not to lose sight of your right to move on. Being left behind can become a kind of purgatory. You exist somewhere between the living still happening here and the loved one who has gone… elsewhere. It is easy to get stuck in this place, and important to do all you can to get past it.

I met someone soon after my husband died. We weren't ever romantically involved, but he listened patiently for hours while I cried about Paul, and I listened to him share trials of losing his brother, who was terminally ill. His brother was forty-seven, the same age as Paul when he died.

This new friend's situation of watching his loved one suffer over many months made me realize that although Paul dying suddenly was absolutely dreadful, it could have been so much worse. I believe I crossed paths with this person at this particular time for a reason. The perspective I gained from supporting him and accepting his support in return made it possible for me to breathe again when it seemed impossible. For that, I will forever be grateful.

In reality, people die young every day. Yes, this fact sucks, and if it happened to someone close to you, that sucks even more. But if you stay in the phase of asking WHY, you cannot recover. Whatever your belief, find a way to somehow make peace with it. It doesn't matter what your faith may or may not be. It doesn't matter how young the departed or how big the scope of the tragedy. Questioning WHY doesn't help. Settle yourself on an answer. Find a reason and some good that may come from it. This takes time, but it is a worthy goal.

I've said to many people that Paul was such a bright light, God needed him in heaven. My youngest son says that heaven must have been short comedians, so his dad was called up! For me, especially in comforting my boys, I needed medical evidence to validate and ground my understanding. I explained to my children that Paul's death saved their lives, because they will always check their hearts and live much longer.

In no way am I saying not to mourn. Of course you will be sad, have terrible moments, and times of sheer heartbreak. I've had all of it and I'm sure I'm not done. My only suggestion here is to find some peace apart from questioning why, if you can.

My younger son and I go over the positives. He says, "Well, I have an iPhone, and I have a new bed and my own room." Then he points out my positives, like that I am home a lot more. Apparently, according to him, all I did before was work. He also lists that I have more time to devote to keeping thin and in shape. I'm not sure if he actually thinks I'm so thin or in shape. Last summer, he commented that my butt was too big to wear a bathing suit in public! You have to love children.

How is having children so much fun? Unless, when they are acting out, you have that mutual look with your partner like, 'this was your idea, *I* never wanted kids!' And you laugh together. I miss laughing with my husband about our boys.

On my worst days, I cry excessively; the opposite of what Paul would want. I know he would be the first one telling me to move on, go out and date, have fun, be happy.

Life is short, LIVE.

On my good days, I try to be happy for Paul. No, he didn't want to leave, but he is at peace now. He no longer carries any earthly worries. He doesn't have to get up for work, figure out how to pay bills, watch when the kids are heartbroken. There are advantages to being dead! And truly loving someone means being happy they're in peace.

A little at a time, the days have grown more bearable. I remember in one of the bereavement groups, someone saying after their spouse was gone for years, "I finally figured out I was a single parent!" I wish my skill at denial was better, because I figured that out after eight hours. No joke.

On my good days, I try to make him proud.

—CHAPTER 9—

WHAT NOT TO DO

You're exhausted, tired, unable to concentrate. Your heart is broken. It isn't easy to sleep. You are immeasurably sad. The last thing you need is a list of instructions, and yet there are certain pitfalls you will be happy to avoid.

Don't make any decisions. My biggest mistake was taking insurance money out when I should have left it in an account earning interest. I was so tired, upset, and angry, then even too tired to be angry. YOU ARE IN A FOG! The fog was the worst two to three months out, and lasted until at least the year anniversary.

I don't remember much of the first year. It's like a blur. I was living on instinct. Don't avoid getting proper rest. I stopped taking naps at eleven months old. Always thought sleep was overrated. Suddenly, for the first time in my life, napping when nothing was going on was exactly what I was doing! I kept saying I was like a dog. When nothing was going on, I was sleeping.

Don't try to put the air conditioners in yourself—not the best idea... but the boys and I did it.

> *Don't avoid asking for help.*
> *ASK FOR HELP!*

I suck at asking for help. Thankfully, people kept helping without me asking. I know this sounds cliché, but people love you and they loved your spouse, they love your children. Let them help. I still suck at this, but there are times when you are at your wit's end and an angel arrives to save the day. Don't fight it. Just say thank you.

Don't put off financial responsibilities. Find someone you trust who is good with paperwork. Make sure they go over what you need to do to settle your loved one's estate. Pay your bills. If you need to borrow money, take out a 0% credit card and survive for a little while. Focus on a simple short-term budget to stay afloat until you can think about the bigger picture.

Finally, don't neglect yourself. The fog was good, I couldn't always feel everything. The downside was, I wasn't tuned in or aware. I gave tons of energy to my children; didn't save much for myself. If you do this, you will burn out. That isn't good for anyone. Don't ignore what your body tells you it needs.

—CHAPTER 10—

UMM, DATING—NOT!

It's funny, my children expected me to find them a new dad in the first few months. When they asked for a new father, I would say, "No problem, there's a DAD aisle at Walmart, I can just go pick one up. What size?" At least it made them laugh for the moment.

John and Mark wanted me to date, and even helped me look at pictures on the websites from time to time. We also googled how to buy a dad, or husband. There are some crazy sites out there; obviously I think they're fake, but they were funny.

Before I embarked on the possibility of dating, I had a sit down with my sons, to explain. It was an interesting conversation. I told them how great artists have depicted romantic love in their works, including: poems, songs, from metal-to-ballads, books, movies, paintings, and sculptures. Many artists and writers have expressed feelings about the topic of love for thousands of years.

I also explained that finding romantic love is an endeavor most people engage in, but even if I find romantic love again, it would in no way change how I feel about their dad. That will never change.

Their responses were priceless. Mark said, "I don't care if you date, Mom, but do I have to go? Because I don't want to go to any boring dinners." Once I assured him that he was off the hook, he was fine with it, and went off to play video games.

John, my older son, said, "It's ok. Since you'll be out more, I can play the drums, right?"

For myself and my children, and even for Paul, I had to make an effort to rebuild my life, including attempting to find romantic love. Dating is part of being a widow that can't be left out or sugar coated.

I tried. I tried to date. For the record, I was on eight dating websites, that I can remember. I met some interesting people. My record was five meetings/dates in a week. Mostly, they were a waste of time.

Please understand, I did my best to listen and be kind to these gentlemen, but simply didn't have the energy. Some men were kind, but there was no attraction. Others were quite attractive, but the foreplay was, "So, are we having sex yet? It's been two hours!"

The more I dated, the worse it was. I wasn't even trying to compare these men to Paul. There was no comparison. Sure, I could go to certain places or keep searching certain sites, but that didn't mean I would meet a man who would be right for me. That is far more up to chance than my controlling nature liked to admit. I could easily have a boyfriend or sex on demand, just not with a person I wanted to be with. Dating itself made me feel like I was sinking. I had no idea what I was doing.

Public Service Announcement: The dating world has changed. I can't compete with women who send naked pictures. More power to you if that makes you happy, but it isn't me. Never will be. I am a lifer. If I have to choose between serial dating for the next twenty years or being alone, I would rather be alone than have what to me would feel like an endless string of awkward encounters.

*We all yearn for safety in
companionship, and seek the
mate we believe is our true match,
somehow believing that taking
certain actions, we can ensure our
safety and control our destinies.
We can't! That's not to say that
we shouldn't strive for our best
in everything we do. Why else
be alive? But to believe that we
have control is the epitome of
narcissism—not just individual
narcissism, but as a species.*

The human brain has an innate capacity to categorize. This is our feeble attempt to find sense in a world that doesn't always make sense. It is one of the ways we attempt to control our environment. Here are my ridiculous, <u>NOT REAL</u> categories for men:

1. Co-dependent
2. Serial daters
3. Cyber-daters

4. Porn addicts
5. Lifers
6. Serial lifers
7. I suspect there is a category of well-adjusted and nor-mal, but I have yet to find it.

Okay, just kidding.

Co-dependent men are fun. After the first date, they may ask you on a weekend trip, need to text incessantly, start asking where you are. You may need to give an itinerary of what you're doing, because if you don't respond, they just keep texting. I also like a prompt response, but find it laborious to keep up the back-and-forth beyond a short exchange.

From my very limited experience, some co-dependent men seem to have issues with substance abuse; either previously married to an alcoholic or substance abuser, or struggling with addiction themselves. I don't judge anyone who fights these battles, but I also don't want anything to do with drugs, and certainly don't want any active substance abusers near my boys. These guys are not for me.

Serial daters. These guys are interesting. Maybe they've never been married, or maybe married multiple times. From the few I've encountered, they seem to have little insight, don't know what they want, end up dating for superficial attraction, having sex, and then only stick with it for a while. They have confessed to me that they usually know it's over way before they leave the relationship. Unfortunately—and I admit this may be unfair—I can't help thinking they're like little boys who always need something new and shiny. I have expressed more than once that since I cannot see an expiration date on my ass, I may not be right for them.

Ah, the cyber-daters. They don't really seem to want to meet. I guess they have virtual relationships because they can be aloof, distant, maybe even intimate from a distance, yet safe. I'm not sure, but believe there may be a correlation between cyber daters and sexting addictions. Just speculation, but I would love to do an experiment to investigate. The few I've met have sent soft porn pictures and flirted a lot. Fun for a bit.

Believe me, my husband and I flirted via text, even the day before he died. However, we actually spent time together, knew each other, had a life together, and texting was only one way we communicated, not the predominant or exclusive way. I started to ask prospective suitors if they wanted to be in the same room with someone having sex or if the phone sexting was enough. UGH!!

Then there are the apparent porn addicts; I say this loosely. In this fake category, I also put the phone sex guys. Yes, the guys you are talking to that break into moans after flirting or sex talk, having an orgasm as they masturbate on the phone with you. Okay, of course I hung up! Then, the others who like to send pornography—not too hardcore, just raunchy enough to test your response. Ah, the digital age!

Please, I would love to say I was a prude. With the right person, someone you are comfortable with, when there is mutual respect for either a one night stand or maybe the love of your life...lots of preferences can fly. Have at it. But a brand new person, practically a stranger, trying to connect by jerking off over the phone? It may work for others. No judgment. But these guys are not for me.

I started wishing I could live carefree and have multiple flings, at least one at a time. I mean, what the hell! I tried, it's not me. Serious disadvantage for a widowed female in the twenty-first century.

Lifers. The definition of a lifer, as I see it, is a hopeless romantic who believes in finding one true love and spending the rest of their lives together. They want to be with someone, bonded and devoted for eternity. I am a lifer. Or, I was. Unfortunately, in some cases, this can be highly connected to co-dependence, see number 1 above.

Serial lifers. I've found that although some say they are lifers, they may actually be lying to themselves, and their dates. They say they want to spend the rest of their life with someone; however, after just a few years, they find the need to look for the next love of their life! Seriously?!

As for well adjusted, normal guys, there seem to be some, but I'm pretty picky. I wasn't attracted to them. I even dated people for other traits when I didn't feel any chemistry or attraction. I did my best to focus on the best in people. It didn't work.

I can't even count how many people have said that I 'will eventually find a nice companion'. I look at them like, if I wanted a companion, I'd get a dog or a cat. I'm not ninety-years-old! I want to fall in love, have great sex, enjoy life; not go to a matinee movie and early bird blue plate special every week!

Recently, a friend told me how hard it would be for them if I found someone. I get it, it is hard after someone dies, to see their widow or widower with someone else. I just keep thinking, *what would Paul want for me? To be alone and unhappy the rest of my life? No way.*

Statistically speaking, I have less than a 15% chance to ever marry again (US Census data, 2015). Obviously, these are census statistics which do not consider common law and long-term commitments, which seem to be more prevalent.

Just for fun, here are some of the best dating lines I've been fed. *THIS IS HYPERBOLE* —slightly exaggerated, but basically true:

"You're pretty and smart. Wow, *girl,* you must get a lot of guys."

"I want to go to Hedonism with you and watch you have sex with other men." *This was on the second and yes, last date.*

"My wife who passed away was about your size. I kept a lot of clothes… Oh, but the shoe size is off." *Can you imagine?*

"Really, do we have to label our relationship? Can't we just have sex?" *Last date, again!*

"How can you break up with me? I'm rich. You are going to struggle financially." *I do think I could get used to not struggling financially, and certainly would like to try it someday! But NOT with you.*

"I like choking women in bed. Does that bother you?" *This was on the first date. Goodbye.*

"I'm going to write a book about online dating. You really meet some weirdos… Can we go out to your car? I am really attracted to you. Want to make out and maybe masturbate?"

"Sorry I'm late." *No problem. I saw you were online, chatting with other women on the same dating website we met on.*

"I think you're an eight and a half!" *If any man is reading this, just say nine. Round up, even if the woman is a freakin five. It will not bode well for you otherwise. I think most married men have figured this out already, but those are the ones who are still married.*

"You look a lot better than your picture!"

In speaking with an English professor, I thought dating him might be intellectually stimulating, interesting, nice. When we started talking about our respective ideas of a perfect date, he said, "Well, how about we get a coffee, and if we hit it off, we can go back to my place and have sex."

"I put I was divorced on the website to be honest, but if I let people know I've been married and divorced three times, who would date me?" *At seventy years old this might be understandable, but at forty? Really?*

I asked one guy, "Why does your picture online look so different?" He answered, "Oh, it's from a while ago." *Like, college?*

My favorite date story since Paul died: I was three weeks out of neck surgery, still wearing a collar. A gentleman from town—cute, funny, divorced, kept asking me out. I knew he had wanted to date me for some time, and told him I wasn't ready. I call him the octopus, for reasons you'll find out in a minute...

We met for drinks and appetizers in a town close by. It was fun and nice. He invited me back to his place for coffee. I love coffee, and I'm an idiot! When we got back to his place, he started kissing me. Seriously, who doesn't want to have a teenage make-out session? I would have so much rather be with Paul, but okay that's not possible.

I'm stupid. I didn't realize that as adults you don't have innocent teenage make-out sessions. Before I knew it, there were hands venturing into places where I was uncomfortable being touched. I was working out, but didn't take Brazilian Jiu Jitsu and was actually laughing out loud while defending my position.

I finally said, "Okay, take your hand off my ass before you lose more than you want to." To which he replied, "We are all adults here."

"Yes, I'm an adult and sure, I like to have sex, but first date, on the couch? I barely know you!" That guy wasn't for me.

I ended up choosing nicknames for the men I dated: the millionaire, the octopus, sonnet man, etc. For me, it wasn't there. Maybe I simply didn't meet the right person, or the men I met didn't view love and marriage the way I do. No one felt like a fit.

I can't recommend dating as a widow. Romantic prospects in this world are unfortunately, a sad state. I can see dating after divorce, but then again, some people are really bitter. I have heard a number of divorce horror stories, and men are pretty angry that they are the ones who have to pay the majority of the money to their ex-spouse (well, according to the men I met.)

If Paul and I had divorced, I would've had to pay and buy him out of my practice. After all, he put me through many years of graduate school. I think he deserved to be bought out. I can't understand the irony of women who believe they should be treated 100% equally, except when obtaining a divorce. I suspect this is a swing back to when women were bought and sold, not that long ago.

As far as the battle of the sexes, I think both sides stink. Men sometimes appear short-sighted, emotionally blunted, stubborn, and ungrateful. Women sometimes appear whiny, angry over nothing, and ungrateful.

Newsflash, there is no battle. Women are treated differently at times and shouldn't be. Men are treated differently sometimes and shouldn't be. It is a well-known scientific fact that males and females are physically different from each other in muscle mass, hormones, and any number of other factors. Unfortunately, not all of the world has caught up to equal treatment. It shouldn't be too complicated to recognize equal value in each person's life while appreciating each other's differences.

While we're on the topic, I can't stand the overzealous efforts for sexes to be considered the same. Men and women are not the same! They should be valued absolutely equally in every sense—professionally, in relationships, by themselves, in daily life and chores, etc. There is no excuse for different pay or opportunities, but equal does not have to mean being the same. Far from it.

I would say I was more accomplished, maybe even smarter than many men I dated. In my experience, the less educated men were on average kinder, and seemed to have more respect for women in general. In contrast, *in my experience*, the very rich men were the worst! Privileged, entitled, obnoxious, arrogant. Still having that locker room mentality, which may be fine as a joke, maybe not, but definitely is not okay in practice.

In my view, women objectify men maybe as much as the other way around, but women may not always act on those thoughts as readily. Then again, of the anecdotal evidence I've collected, more women cheated on their husbands than men were unfaithful to their wives. I only came in contact with a sample of the population, but it's pretty clear the times have changed, and it remains to be seen if these changes have left us—men OR women—happier in the dating world.

> TANGENT: *To be honest,*
> *I'm confused about gender wars.*
> *So much fuss about men vs. women,*
> *sexual preferences, gender identity.*
> *It all seems pretty simple to me.*
> *Each individual has the right*
> *to pursue happiness as long*
> *as they do not hurt anyone.*
> *My goodness,*
> *live and let live, and shut up.*

After all the dating sites and meetups, the only man I called by name was the one friend I mentioned earlier, the man I got close to right after losing Paul. He and I went on countless faux dates, flirted some, and spoke all the time on the phone. Over the course of many months and the subsequent passing of his brother, we developed a rare, precious bond that would be tough to break. He is good looking, funny, and sweet, but for any number of reasons, we keep a mutual understanding to remain platonic friends. Sometimes it has felt like falling in love, but we've never had a physical relationship. We are intimately connected because we supported each other through the worst year of our lives. He has been a blessing for me, and I have no regrets.

When I look back, I think I simply wasn't ready to date. I tried desperately, thinking it would help me to find someone, because being in love helps make life worthwhile, and time is passing.

This brings me to a problem I don't know if other people discuss. Until the day he died, I looked at Paul like he was twenty-six years old. Sure, I guess he had gained weight, had some gray hair, etc. but to me, he was my absolutely beautiful husband.

Even when I got to the hospital and the doctor came out from behind the curtain to let me know my husband had died, I repeatedly said, "My beautiful husband is dead, my beautiful husband is dead." I'm angry and sad that I never get that again; angry and sad that no one else will look at me like I'm twenty-five years old forever. I hate that about being a widow. I hate that dating now means starting from scratch in my forties.

> ## "A *thing of beauty is a joy forever*"
> —John Keats

Even as I say that, I realize how lucky I was to have found real love for twenty-one years. My love with Paul will forever be that, despite its imperfections, a thing of beauty and joy.

—CHAPTER 11—

WHAT PEOPLE
FAIL TO MENTION

S ome people think death is contagious. Okay, I'm joking. Sort of.

Some friends and relatives can't handle what happened and avoid you as much as possible. It's a fact. This happened to me and to my children, even with friends who were close prior to Paul's death. Mark's best friend for years simply couldn't deal with the pain we were all experiencing. He didn't know how to handle the changes in Mark. He basically no longer could be friends with Mark. This was another loss and heartbreak at the worst possible time; horrible for Mark and monumentally difficult to watch as a parent.

People don't want to talk about death. Some think if they bring it up, they may be depressing the very person they are trying to comfort. Listen, if you're the person with the loss, it's usually on your mind anyway. People may think that you should be over it already. "Well it's been a year, two years…" They have no idea how grief works.

Time doesn't actually HEAL the wound. You just learn to manage and cope better as months and years pass. The pain of loss doesn't go away. Hopefully, you incorporate ways to deal with it differently and live your life.

The other thing no one talks about is that I now do everything by myself. I know this came up earlier and it will keep coming up again. It is the most surreal thing, after being with someone and living each day and night with them for twenty+ years. People think it's over, like you can forget, but my other half is *still* missing, whether I like it or not.

My parents and siblings do their best, but aren't able to help often. My friends work full time. I have carpools, but no real help. Yes, I hire help when I go to work or when I attempt to go out. What else can I do? People forget that you are managing alone every day. They take for granted that even if they don't usually hire help, they have it right there next to them.

Some of my friends' husbands do far less than they do. I know that exists. However, if they need a ride for the kids, want to go to a nighttime event, need to travel for work, have an appointment on a Saturday morning, their husbands can step up. They are right there in the house. God forbid if these women are hurt or sick, their husbands can take over. I'm not saying their significant others are perfect, but their children are fed and their households still run—albeit maybe at a bare minimum—without them. That is no longer possible for a widow.

I don't know how to be a baseball dad, who to talk to or not during baseball tryouts, bowling tryouts, how to deal with coaches. I suck at this! That's today, not three or four years ago. It's real right now. Regardless of whether it's fair or not, I'm in it alone.

I've driven myself to the hospital, taken a taxi alone when for medical reasons you're not supposed to, been alone in the emergency room for hours with problems related to my autoimmune disease. I've stayed in the hospital alone (sometimes it's actually more peaceful). In the big scheme of things, maybe it's no big deal, but it is different and not something I'm totally used to yet. Even so, it's much easier now than the first year or two.

Another hushed subject... Not all wives want an okay-looking single woman/widow around their husbands. I heard rumors and I've gotten looks. Most of these women barely want their husbands themselves. I thought it was hysterical that they thought I suddenly wanted them. Seriously, when this happened, I wanted to show Paul's picture and then list his attributes like a resume. For one thing, I was way too self-confident to be fourth or fifth on someone's list, and for another, I would NEVER date a married man! Not happening, not me. I have such a reverence for the sanctity of marriage, it wouldn't even cross my mind.

Actually, when Paul was alive, tons of married women confessed to me that they had a crush on him; he had that 'je ne se qua'. Paul constantly and quite innocently flirted with women, all women. I thought it was sweet. Sometimes, he would come home from work and describe a beautiful woman he had seen that day. I thought, *great, it doesn't matter to me where your appetite comes from, as long as you come home for dinner*. And he did. We were committed to each other.

As a widow, I have often not been invited places because people didn't know if, how, or where I would fit in. Most functions and gatherings are all couples. This wasn't meant to be mean; it was actually just uncomfortable for people. I got used to it, and with my family and close friends it isn't an issue. Since I'm being so honest, I'll just put this out there.

The first year is terrible, and the second year is worse. The first year, you're in a fog. I don't know if everyone feels the same way, but from my anecdotal interviews, it's what I have gathered. I felt all the time like I had left something at home, like there was a vacancy in my soul, a yearning that will never be satisfied.

Paul and I had different interests, different likes and dislikes. We were two independent people; not connected at the hip. Nonetheless, I still feel like I lost half of myself when he died. The solace of his heartbeat, the total acceptance in his love, that's irreplaceable.

It's funny, when I discuss this with people—sometimes prospective dates—many have no clue. Many say, "I never felt like that…" which makes me wonder why they ever got married in the first place! No wonder it didn't work out.

So, is true love a fairy tale? Do we delude ourselves into thinking it's real?

Paul and I bickered. I couldn't stand him some days, but

we were lifers... I would have been more than happy to grow old with him. People talk about settling, but we are ALL less than perfect. The goal, if there is one, is to find our unique perfect match, our soul mate. How can people date if they don't even think like this? If you are seeking perfection and believe you are settling if you don't find it, don't get married.

Struggle kept Paul and I together. The difficult times we survived together gave us perspective on what mattered most. We owned a house when I started graduate school. It was wonderful to get creative together, managing our budget because we had no extra money. We took our bikes to the beach and walked on the boardwalk, and bought our clothes on sale at the cheapest stores. One year we made ornaments out of bows from the 99-cent store for our very sad Christmas tree. I still smile thinking about those times. Does that exist anymore? I can truly say, I don't think it's easy to find.

—CHAPTER 12—

CLOSING REFLECTIONS

One day, my younger son asked, "Mom, how come I can't only see a half-moon anymore? Why am I able to see the full moon when only half is lit up?" "The same reason you can't get toothpaste back in the tube—once it's out, it's out. Once you see or live it, it can't be changed or put back."

I think of this regarding my children. No matter how hard I've worked to maintain stability and security, a normal safety that many kids take for granted is no longer there for my sons. A person they loved dearly is gone. They will miss him forever. I can't ever change that.

Every holiday, birthday, and special occasion changes. From now on there will always be tears of both sadness and happiness, because for the rest of your life and the children's lives, you mourn that their other parent isn't there. It never ends.

On my son's sixteenth birthday, I cried every second he wasn't around for twenty-four hours. He cried too, saying, "I thought Dad was going to take me to DMV for my permit, teach me to drive, go to the rock concert with me." What can I say to that? I just supported him, cried with him, and promised to do absolutely anything I could to make his birthday special.

My older one figured out how to shave on his own. These are bittersweet moments as we miss their dad and yet, one day at a time, find our way without him.

Things haven't been quite as bad recently as the first two to three years. I still cry often, and despite knowing that my husband would want me to live fully and move on, I wonder if I'm not just waiting to see him again. My answer came in a fortune cookie one day. It said, "Who are you to decide fate, fate decides for you."

I realize that all of my fears, wants, dreams, and nightmares don't matter. I just have to plow through the way I always have, like a bull in a china shop. If things are going to get messy, I will simply keep cleaning up! I have no choice, even if I wish for something else. My boys need me, and being a mom overpowers all else. This is a good thing, a blessing.

When all else fails, I have so much hope for my boys. Paul was an amazing person. He had a great personality that drew people to him. He was humble, kind, gracious, and sweet. He was indeed a survivor of a very tough childhood, and overcame so much. John and Mark have half of his genetic makeup. I can't wait to see how they turn out. I have hope for my children to build and enjoy great lives, to marry people they are madly in love with, and to be happy. I believe this is possible. Life is beautiful now, even without Paul.

Just take a breath. Life is beautiful now because we are here and the sun shines, the moon glows, and the stars twinkle. We exist and that may have to be enough.

Admittedly, life was better with the love we shared. No doubt, my life now is less colorful, but I am blessed with the gift of memories, laughter, and what he would say at any moment that still rings in my head. That part hasn't ended, and that's wonderful.

I waited to publish this book, thinking at some point there would be a happy ending to my story. I was hoping it would close like a fairy tale. I could meet a handsome, sweet, good-hearted millionaire and we'd fall madly in love; or maybe my 'friend' decides he can't live without me, professes his love, proposes, and we have a beautiful wedding and life together. I might find a dream job that pays a ton of money for minimal work. (Wait, don't we all dream this?!) Maybe I win LOTTO…

None of these outcomes have happened (so far) and I have given up on dating (for now). What I've learned is that there is no ending until we cease to wake up. Every day is a beginning, even the days that start with tears.

I still miss Paul terribly. My boys speak about not recalling his voice. They ask me what he would have wanted for them. My answer is true, clear, and simple, "for you to find love, to live and be happy."

That's what I hope for them, too. I know I will enjoy every goal they achieve. I love seeing them smile, hearing them giggle, or hearing them sing a tune when they think I'm not listening. I still laugh out loud and smile from my heart when telling them stories about their dad.

As for me, I'm not sure what my life will be like two, five, or ten years from now. I'm grateful for my children, my friends, my family, my job, the gym, chocolate, my very wonderful car, and my lovely, quaint home. I hope those pieces of my life and my gratitude for twenty-one years of love with Paul will carry me through whatever comes next.

I hope I continue to live in the moment, smile at strangers, and make others smile the way Paul did. Most of all, I hope I make him, and myself, proud of me; maybe not every day, but most days.

EPILOGUE

I'm a scientist. I think it's fun to focus on what others might find boring. For example, subatomic particles. There is evidence that once a subatomic particle 'entangles' with another, they can have an effect on each other when separated by great distances. If one intertwined particle moves, even thousands of miles away, the other particle moves as well. We are, in essence, made up of subatomic particles, so are we humans that different? Or can we sometimes stay connected in a way we don't yet see?

WHAT YOU NEED TO DO
BUT DON'T WANT TO

I suggest keeping the following in a notebook or in notes on your phone or computer with a secure backup for easy reference. You can also give it to a trustworthy friend or relative. This is in no way an exhaustive list; it is what I had to do! I hope this will help you avoid some unnecessary stress and feel better prepared to face each day.

DATES & DEADLINES

Check to be certain you are NOT missing important dates. It's hard to concentrate and think, but you must make sure you meet certain deadlines, especially for life and health insurance. Have a friend or relative help you go down the annual checklist and mark dates with alarm reminders on your preferred device calendar.

DEATH CERTIFICATE

Get a batch of official copies of the death certificate; you'll need it for everything. If the cause of death is uncertain, you may want to order more death certificates. Obtain extra copies once the cause of death is revealed. I called the Medical Examiner's office regularly to find out the cause of death; I needed to know.

WILL

- If there was no will and you and your spouse/partner were living together in good standing, e.g., not legally separated or divorced, as the spouse, in many states, you are entitled to their belongings.

- Get your own Will to ensure that all of your assets are covered. If you have children, you need to ensure that their guardians are named in your own Will. Believe it or not, I spoke openly about this with my children so they knew there was a plan, even though it was not going to happen.

ESTATE

- Settle the estate or whatever is left as quickly as you can. Consult an estate lawyer and begin the probate process if required.

- Keep an estate account in your loved one's name open for as long as possible. Checks come in your loved one's name for a long time.

INSURANCE

If you get insurance money, make sure you speak to a capable and trustworthy financial advisor about what to do with it. Insurance policies are designated only to the assigned beneficiaries.

SOCIAL SECURITY

- Obtain Social Security Benefits if you need them. Bring everything: birth certificates, marriage certificates, death certificate, social security cards for everyone involved, including your loved one who died.

- I obtained LifeLock on all of our Social Security numbers because these numbers were all over the place. You may be able to do this for free on a credit site like Credit Karma.

FINANCIALS

- Change accounts into your name and pay your bills! I know, it is so overwhelming, but you cannot ruin your credit score now. Ask for help!

- Get a credit card in your name, not connected to anyone else.

- I know it's too early to think about; however, if you plan to remarry, you have to look into what happens financially. Upon remarrying, even with a prenuptial agreement, I could still lose a third to a half of whatever I had. Protect yourself so you have peace of mind, whatever may follow.

HOME OWNERSHIP & TITLE

- If you own a house, find out how the title is written and if applicable, ask how to get the title changed to your name. We owned very little except my husband's classic car, which wasn't worth enough to go to probate court. In our case, I had to go to a government agency with his will, the title, my marriage certificate, and the death certificate, and the title for the car was changed to my name.

- Many people who own a house have insurance to pay off the house mortgage. Do this if you can, or if trusted advisors tell you to.

BENEFITS

Are you entitled to a pension? If your spouse had a traditional job with benefits, be sure to speak with their Human Resources department.

- Confirm the continuation of your spouse's health insurance.

- Or, if you held the insurance on a policy in your name, it probably won't have to change.

- Find out if your spouse had a 401k, IRA, or any retirement investment accounts from other institutions. If you intend to use this money, it has to be deposited into an inherited account. Typically you will have to take distributions each year. If it doesn't go into the correct account, you won't have access without a significant penalty, so make sure you check instructions and place funds in the correct account for easy access with minimal or no penalties.

DENTAL INSURANCE

UGH…If you were lucky enough to have this and can afford to keep it on Cobra, decide if you want to use it. If not, make sure you look into dentists and see if you can obtain a discount plan with payment options BEFORE you lose the benefit.

SECURITY & SAFETY

- My children were young, so I decided to get a cheap alarm system on the house. They played baseball, so I always had bats nearby... just in case.

- People are easily scammed at times like this! Financial companies, charities, fake causes... be aware and on alert for mail or phone calls you don't recognize. People prey on the vulnerable, so you have to be careful!

- Even or especially on dating sites, there are people who prey on lonely hearts. Make sure friends always know who you are with, where you are going to meet, and the name of the person you are seeing. Do NOT get in a car with anyone until you know and trust them, and make a mental note of any distinguishing appearance details.

YOUR CHILDREN'S MENTAL HEALTH

You'll have to inform the school. I made a plan with the principal so that my children could go to the school psychologist or social worker during the day if they needed to.

YOUR MENTAL HEALTH

Make sure someone is going through the mail coming in, talking to the place of work of your loved one, looking into bank accounts and investments of any kind, or looking into debt, and what you have to do. It all feels impossible to think about when you are trying to get through each day, so choose one or two relatives or friends you can trust to help you.

HELPFUL SITES
& RESOURCES

L ook up what actually happened to your spouse. Whether the death of your spouse was due to a tragic event, or a long-term or short-term illness, there is often a helpful site or support group you can join. Below are some books, links and resources.

24/7 SUPPORT

My Grief Angels
www.mygriefangels.org

Grief Anonymous Facebook Group
www.griefanonymous.com/facebook-groups/

WEBSITES

Heart Links Grief Center
www.myheartlinks.com

Grief & Creativity
www.griefandcreativity.com

Open to Hope
www.opentohope.com

TAPS
Grief Support for Military Families
www.taps.org

Unspoken Grief
Support for Families Who Have Lost Babies
www.unspokengrief.com

Grieving
Grief Support Forums
www.forums.grieving.com

Friends Along The Road

Grief Support Programs, Articles & Discussion Groups

www.friendsalongtheroad.org

Recover From Grief

Archive of Resources

www.recover-from-grief.com

Dougy

Center for Grieving Children and Families

www.dougy.org

READING

It's Grief by Edy Nathan

OTHER RESOURCES

BEREAVEMENT GROUPS
- Your place of worship
- Local hospitals

CHILDREN SUPPORT GROUPS
There are camps and free support groups for children available by state.

WIDOWED PARENTS FINANCIAL SUPPORT
There are scholarships and financial help for widowed parents to help pay for extracurricular activities for children. You can start at the coach or school level and look into local town, county, state, or private institution programs.

This is just enough to get you started on finding the resources that may be right for you. On my website www. bellalynnthompson.com I will continue to add additional resources and offer helpful tips and ideas to get you through what I know is a really difficult time in your life. I hope you'll connect with me there or on social media.

REFERENCES

Keats, J., & Buckland, W. J. (1947). *Endymion: A poetic romance*. London: Printed at the Golden Cockerel Press.

Naito, R.A. (Producer) and McGrath, T. (Director). (2017). *The Boss Baby*. U.S.A. Produced by DreamWorks Animation and distributed by 20th Century Fox. United States Census Data. 2015. Retrieved

ACKNOWLEDGEMENTS

I wanted to acknowledge Beth Kallman Werner of Author Connections, LLC for her incredible editing magic and unending kindness and support. In addition, Marina Aris of Brooklyn Writers Press for her input that greatly improved this book. Lastly, I'd like to thank all who supported me through this publishing process.

ABOUT THE AUTHOR

Bella Lynn Thompson has drafted the ultimate labor of love. A life-long writer she turned to the page to grieve and make sense of her loss following the death of her husband. In her debut book, 'Sudden Widow, A True Story of Love, Grief, Recovery, and How Badly It Can Suck!' she recounts her happiest and most trying times, and through her words manages to find a way to offer guidance and support to other widows.

Bella graduated with a PhD. in Psychology and has worked as a psychologist in multiple settings, including supervising in a hospital and private practice. She is also a Senior Adjunct Professor of Psychology. On both good days, and bad days, she is a devoted mom to her sons.

www.bellalynnthompson.com

Thank You for Reading

Sudden Widow
A True Story of Love, Grief,
Recovery & How Badly It Can Suck!

If you enjoyed this book, please consider leaving
a short review on your website of choice.

Reviews help both readers and writers.
They are an easy way to support good work and help to
encourage the continued release of quality content.

Connect with Bella Lynn Thompson
www.bellalynnthompson.com

Want the latest from the Brooklyn Writers Press?

Browse our complete catalog.
www.brooklynwriterspress.com